# Ghosts in Time
# and Space

Douglas Richardson

# Also by Douglas Richardson

*Poems for Loners*

*The Corruption of Zachary R.*

*Out in the Cold, Cold Day*

*Sugar Fish*

# Ghosts in Time
# and Space

Douglas Richardson

Weak Creature Press
Los Angeles

**Ghosts in Time and Space**
©2011 by Douglas Richardson
Weak Creature Press
First Printing, July 2011

All rights reserved. No part of this book may be used or reproduced in any manner whatsoever without written permission from the author except in the case of brief quotations embodied in critical articles or reviews.

This is a work of poetry and fiction. Any resemblance to actual persons, living or deceased, events, or locations is entirely coincidental.

Library of Congress Control Number: 2011933901
ISBN: 978-0-9842424-4-3

Printed in the United States of America.

Cover design by Heather DeSerio, Precision Edge Design LLC.

Author photo by Jen Cairns.

For information on other publications available from Weak Creature Press, please email weakcreature@aol.com.

# Introduction

This collection evokes the sensation of walking through a deserted mining town or stumbling upon an abandoned house, filled with the mysterious yet intimate effects of long-dead strangers. These are poems from the point of view of ghosts. When read individually, each poem stands alone with sharp, imagistic recollections of a life, but when read as a collection, narrative threads emerge, such as that of a brother and sister who were killed in an airplane crash or of a mother and child who lived their brief lives in a hippie commune. These characters fade in and out of the collection, haunting each other's memories and popping up in unexpected places. Many of these ghosts are confined to a single location, like the man who must spend eternity at Los Angeles International Airport, and likewise, many of the poems begin and end with the same line, evoking the feeling of being trapped in a temporal loop, unable to move on. Richardson's voice is darkly humorous, shot through with vivid rays of mournful beauty. In *Ghosts in Time and Space*, he has channeled the poetic voices of characters who wander between this world and the next. They may be invisible, voiceless and unreal, but their desire to tell their stories feels very human, and very real indeed. As Richardson puts it, in the voice of a seraph: "I am silent, not songless."

—Ana Reyes, poet

# Contents

The First True Breath ............................ 1
Rattle ...................................................... 3
Kept Low ................................................ 4
Bakersfield ............................................. 5
A New Town ........................................... 6
The Seraph ............................................. 7
Mimeograph ........................................... 8
Scorn ..................................................... 10
3:36 ....................................................... 11
Spectrum .............................................. 12
A Lifetime of Temporary Philosophies ... 13
Paragenesis .......................................... 14
The Staircase ....................................... 16
Hollywood Bowl ................................... 18
Death March ........................................ 19
Lost Hours ............................................ 20
Movements .......................................... 23
Endless Loop ....................................... 25
Corona .................................................. 26
The Scarecrow ..................................... 27

| | |
|---|---|
| Friction Match | 28 |
| Devil Holding a Highball | 29 |
| Blind Eyes | 30 |
| Dual | 32 |
| Duello | 34 |
| Becoming | 36 |
| A Serious Boy | 38 |
| Grand Transformation | 39 |
| Journeyman | 41 |
| Inheritance | 42 |
| Because | 43 |
| Ascension | 45 |

*for all groundwarmers,
past and present*

# The First True Breath

My finest day as a groundwarmer
was the day I ceased to be one
a passing through
upon the miracle of death
which we all agree
was the first true breath

Ghosts, show them your stories
your poetic failures
your prosaic glories
frighten them if you must

Prove to them their waning faith
may be rekindled by a wraith

# Rattle

In the world I come from
we fall in love only once.

This does not mean mistakes
are not made
or are infrequent.

Our population is small
like your Wyoming,
and like Wyoming
the living and the deceased
haunt the land with equal skill.

Our world is cool and green
and our architects
are quite accomplished.

I don't travel much to other worlds;
I prefer to work like the bees
in our vast gardens,
as vast as your oceans.

Occasionally I rattle
a child's cup of cider;
this small thrill for the child
reminds me of my mistake.

## Kept Low

When I died, I asked to see Jesus
so I was sent to the Holy Land
during his time on earth.

I was ashamed and kept low in the Jordan
which pleased him,
and he filled me with his spirit
which made me cry.

His followers on the riverbank heard me
but because I was low
they thought I was a ripple in the water.

# Bakersfield

One morning I opened the newspaper
and saw the doe eyes of a drifter
who had passed away
on the side of a highway
near Bakersfield.

The photo had been taken
two years earlier
and was the last known
image of the man.

I never spoke again
for the rest of my days,
which really wasn't much of a feat
since I only lived another week.

When I was alive, I would have
passed him by with mean eyes.

This hurts my core even now.

I am desperate to find this man.

A newspaper blowing along the highway
in Bakersfield
means I am looking.

## A New Town

In the city I searched
for a solitary painting,
a rain-blackened tree.
I held hot water in a paper cup,
avoided the hostile eyes of strangers.
Later I left town.
Long grass grew in the gravel
and made the sky turn gray.
Tar on telephone poles –
warm to the touch.
And then open desert.
Transmission towers stretched
into the distance,
past where I could see.
And then night –
almost black, with no mind.
Sleep was the strange night event.
Later I arrived in a new town.

# The Seraph

I am the seraph in the faraway blue
I am 45 degrees Fahrenheit
give or take one or two
I am silent, not songless
I am disarming and miraculous
How can stars speak intimately
yet somehow they do
I am the seraph in the faraway blue

# Mimeograph

When I was young I was drawn to books,
but I had a different reason.

It began in kindergarten
in the time of the mimeograph.
The teacher would go desk to desk
passing out paper warm with purple ink,
which the kids pressed against their noses
to inhale the mild chemicals.

A lifetime as a connoisseur of book scents
came to an end
and I found myself in an open field
with bookshelves stretching
beyond the horizon.

I cracked open the first book
and was greeted with a burst of lilacs.
How peculiar, I thought.
Then I noticed something else
about the book:
The pages were blank,
all of them.

I pulled another book off the shelf, *Skunk*,
which evoked memories
of my honeymoon in the forest;
and another, *Patchouli*,
which reminded me of my anxiety;

and another, *Creation*,
which smelled like California after rain.

When I was young I was drawn to books,
but I had a different reason.

## Scorn

for protection I kept a rusty nail
in a beat-up Betty Boop tote bag
and twirled my frizzy hair;
barnacles under the boardwalk
made me cry

my goal early in life was to spot
the farthest point I could see
and run away from it

my goal late in life was to return
to where I came from
using beer and antihistamines

drug-softened memories were so quiet
they kept me company
like faraway islands
and the
silent ocean between

## 3:36

I lived my entire life in a hippie commune.
I don't have much to say about it,
but this doesn't mean I was dull
or without conviction.

I was born three months premature.
My mom ate poison mushrooms
and drank Southern Comfort
because she thought it would
make her more like Janis Joplin.

She was right.
Her singing voice improved
when she was hallucinating and drunk.

The commune midwife who delivered me
believed it wise to play music
for the mother-to-be in labor.
She played Janis Joplin, Neil Young,
the Byrds, and Led Zeppelin.

I came out of my mother's womb
to Zeppelin's "Going to California,"
a pretty song for acoustic guitar
three minutes and thirty-six seconds long.

When the song came to an end, so did I.
My mother followed the next day.
I lived my entire life in a hippie commune.

## Spectrum

Poison mushrooms grew
on Damp Mountain
like quarter notes
and half notes
and whole,
so we ate them
and they made us
sing colors
all the way down
to the Bay:
red and orange,
gold and violet,
even S.F.P.D. blue,
which used its envy against us,
turned us green in the City
and made us impossible to hide.

My comrades and me and the boy in my belly
slept in jail that night, but justice in the morning
brought us back to Damp Mountain, which
trembled and flooded when my water broke.

My girlfriend played music from high above and I
sank into the canyon of birth. Black hours passed,
and then came white silence, and now I am mist
on Damp Mountain.

# A Lifetime of Temporary Philosophies

Mine was a lifetime of temporary philosophies, such as "allow your enemies to laugh in a crowd" or "a case of Budweiser is a portly witch" or "there is so much evil now, we can't even trust the tap water" or "you can't commit suicide if you don't exist."

Voltaire had an aphorism of his own: "A witty saying proves nothing." This, ironically, was my favorite. Somehow I knew I was no more than a pigeon with a human head, or vice versa.

And somehow my shaky religions and my beer left me hazy and bitter. I began voting Republican. I got sober and went back to school. I secured a steady job. Bought a small house. Raked leaves. Talked to my plaid-shirted neighbor.

But eventually this also left me hazy and bitter, and vaguely suicidal, so I abandoned all and just kept on living right through death, finally understanding that life was not mine to take.

## Paragenesis

My sister had a brood
I was barren
she was my tenant
I had her evicted

along with everyone else in the building
whom I deemed could breed

Then I lived alone
twenty-one doors
with twenty-one locks and keys

I gardened on my knees
among the toys and around the swings
that I made her abandon

At night I swung in the moonlight
watching the toys leap and roll
among my roses

Whose invisible brood could this be?
I wondered
and I tamped
their cuts and gashes
when they snagged the thorns

Then one morning
I woke with a strange head
that heard strange horns

and I stayed in bed
until the sun went down

At night I swing in the moonlight
with my visible brood

twenty-one children
with twenty-one locks and keys

## The Staircase

bicycles, carriages, cable cars
anything to be in motion
anything to escape my mortal heft

a staircase in a turn-of-the-century apartment
in San Francisco
narrow and musty
with doors at the top and bottom

no one loitered there
ladies didn't linger
all defensive and mysterious
there was no railing for men
to lean on and leer

this was a tunnel for travel
that echoed after each footfall
as if someone was right on your heels
or closer
as if someone was trying to invade you

I lived in the room behind the top door
until 1906
when the building and I
went down in the quake
a new building went up in 1912
an exact replica of the old one
it is still there today

I am there too
right on your heels
or closer
in the staircase

## Hollywood Bowl

I reside at the Hollywood Bowl
on a summer evening
a helicopter high above and ascending
crickets on the perimeter and
the orchestra forever tuning

the audience is filing in
on the wind
on the wine
on their blankets

the symphony will not begin
until the last one is in
the orchestra forever tuning
a helicopter high above and ascending

## Death March

His beard reminded me of the Civil War
and did we fight together
or against each other
or was it the photograph I once saw
left behind on a bench
along the fringe of the carnival
or the mannequin
in the fortune-teller machine
saying I fought lions 2,000 years ago
or the time I saved the life of a con man
who took all my money
or stopped a rape in progress
or spent the night in jail
for screaming at a crowd of innocents
or drank and drank warm whiskey
and marched and marched
until I was gunned down
in the hot dirt of a Virginia battlefield
or was it a Las Vegas parking lot

## Lost Hours

I get a little choked up in the casino, but I suppress the sound with shrimp cocktail and Heineken, and then I get that feeling that I'm not really here, only to reappear a minute, an hour, sometimes days later at a blackjack table or roulette wheel.

Sometimes I get caught looking into mirrors with the cigarette girls. People think I'm some sort of creep, but I have to look long and deep to keep from disappearing.

I had to come to Vegas. I have to drink and gamble and whore. These activities require persistent attention. They keep me present more than anything else I've tried.

And sometimes I get lucky. Take the other night, for example. I was tossed into a trunk and driven out to Tonopah after I tried to pawn a watch I won a while back. Nice watch, but I got tired of having evidence of my lost hours wrapped around my wrist.

Bouncing on a spare tire for 200 miles also requires persistent attention. So does being buried alive. Funny how I don't disappear when I really need to.

I try not to dwell on that night. I'm still around, after all, and nothing has changed except for the dust in my lungs.

✡

# Movements

groundwarmers in cars and
buses and trains
go from home to work and back again
ghosts through portals in time and walls
move through paintings in museum halls

stare at a painting with intensity
to spot ghosts on the go
catch Proust and his bossy great-aunt
in the clouds of "Woman with Parasol"
see Monet appear in a Pissarro
studying the colors in the streets below

the painters where
rue Saint Vincent meets
rue des Saules
were masters of great renown
their ghosts mimic groundwarmers
trudging their way through town
satisfied by the bump and strain

## Endless Loop

from the satisfied rows of houses
I am separate in my car
listening to Pearl Jam
in the CD player
over and over

stuck in an endless loop
in 1992
when everything seemed to detach
and drift until I decided
under the intensity of emptiness

to drive forever through
the loneliest year
of my life,
which I miss
as if I were not still here

## Corona

I always forgot about
the return of April
when I had to hear
that certain Doors song
about the mist burning off
and the mist returning
simultaneously
in two realms
those thirty
incomprehensible days
undeniable
palpable
the Easter clouds
asleep
and awake

## The Scarecrow

I live in a field where darkness grows
we don't speak of immortality

Where has the light gone?
to the heavens, I suppose
and isn't that just vanity

But I've still got heroin, my
romantic heroine
and I've still got suicide, my
glamorous suicide
and I can still bring myself
to sing
in the shadows
with the crows

I live in a field where darkness grows
we don't speak of immortality

## Friction Match

I hated how the drunkards
scared the children,
so now I scare the drunkards.
I flit by at the outermost reach
of their peripheral vision
and I scream at them.

They flail their arms;
they scream back;
they convince themselves
that I am not there.

And I'm not—
not really.

I'm only truly present afterward
when I spot a gull in the sky.

I hated how the drunkards
scared the children.
I hate that I can no longer get drunk.

## Devil Holding a Highball

Every anniversary my wife and I
went to the same café,
a hint of cinnamon above the candlelight.

Then one anniversary she walked out
the back door and never came back.

Fifty years have passed
since I died.
I've spent each one guessing
where she might have gone,
each scenario more lurid than the last.

In the café is a poster of the devil
holding a highball.
I peer out of his eyes
as if I had his heat
and I watch the nights unfold.

I feel so violent inside
as if I had his eyes
as if I had his heat
and I wonder if I'm in hell.

## Blind Eyes

Worst of all were the blind eyes of the doctors and nurses at the institutions where I spent most of my life. They would shove their degrees in my face and tell me I didn't see what I saw, as if sitting in a classroom acquiring dubious knowledge for eight years made their collective opinion of what I did or didn't see more valid than my own.

It all started when I was a little girl. I pointed at the clear night sky and asked my father if we could go to the carnival. What carnival? he would ask, concerned that I was pointing at the sky. You can imagine where the rest of this conversation led.

And there were other observations and conversations and treatments. I showed a condescending nurse a rock that contained an entire city. This led to electroshock therapy. I told a patronizing doctor I could see air. This led to heavy sedatives and antipsychotics.

I am still unsure how or when I arrived, but I am here (I must be), exactly where I pointed when I was a girl.

I am the lone human specter, which has been agreeable. Alien eyes can see. I show them my father in distant stardust. They see him and agree that he must see me.

## Dual

My eternal residence is
Los Angeles International Airport
I watch the planes take off
I watch the planes land
and besides that I amuse myself
by sliding down the luggage chutes
and flying the lengths of long corridors

There is no weather to distract me
from my placid mood
though I do like to look out
the windows on stormy days

I also like to hold
the passengers' coffee cups
and imagine the warmth
which I can no longer feel

I drank coffee until my 53rd birthday
which was the day I arrived

My sister died in a plane crash
when I was a boy
I never got to know her properly
because we were so young

My eternal residence is
Los Angeles International Airport
I watch the planes take off

I watch the planes land
and I wait for my sister

## Duello

The adults called us the two translucent kids from the neighborhood. They said we had that otherworldly quality which would bring either great fortune or senseless tragedy.

My little brother and I were embarrassed by these grandiose observations. We knew we weren't the kids who would go out into the world and accomplish things or die trying. We weren't the kids who "knew" things. We wondered where knowledge came from, how people understood what to do in the physical world, which baffled the two of us.

That's why I confess I felt relieved when the DC-10 began its terminal descent into the Pacific Ocean twenty miles off the coast of Los Angeles. The anxiety over what I would fail to become vanished. Perhaps I was meant to become a child air crash victim.

I suspect my brother had similar feelings, though the postcrash effects on us have been curiously different. I am able to discern where my brother is and what he is thinking and doing at all times, and I have total recall of our lives and how they ended. My brother, however, thinks he lived to be 53 years old. The life he imagines he lived is so extraordinary that I am still undecided whether I should ever see him again.

My eternal residence is the flight paths and jet streams over California. His eternal residence is Los Angeles International Airport.

## Becoming

I awake on a stranger's lawn
in the Coachella Valley.
It's March 14, 2011.
Eighty-eight degrees will be the high.
The residents pass over
and through me and don't notice.
I should tell you this is not unusual.

I stand and walk to a bus stop,
no hunger and no thirst.
I see migrating geese cutting
in sharp formations,
becoming a school of fish in the sky.
I should tell you this is not possible.

The bus rides through five cities
along the base of the mountains,
past repeating resorts and cafés
and restaurants.
I stop in the same café in three different cities
because I like a room full of voices
other than my own.
I should tell you that I want to live again.

In the evening a brother and sister
play cards on a table outside,
no sound and nothing to burn.
I watch them from an empty parking lot

where the heat of the day still rises.
I should tell you that I rise along with it.

## A Serious Boy

My aunts brought me
to Disneyland
when I was five.
I held tight
to the string
on my balloon,
but it slipped away when
I forgot about it.
I looked up in time
to see it disappear
into the sky.
I became a serious boy
after that day.
My aunts didn't seem
to understand
that I had died.

## Grand Transformation

I won't get into the grisly details except to say that I was a schemer and that one of my many schemes got me killed.

When I died, I heard a voice say you can be anywhere you please, but the first place you think of is where you'll spend eternity.

I thought of the Grand Canyon, which was surprising considering I had never been there and was terrified of heights. It made no sense, as if the thought had been forced on me.

So there I was, perched somewhere on the North Rim in the moonlight, my legs dangling a mile above the river, and I started bargaining with the voice that put me there.

"There must be some kind of mistake," I thought.

"I've never been here before, so I wouldn't have, I couldn't have, thought of this place. You must have misunderstood. I really thought 'Grand Cayman,' not 'Grand Canyon.' "

This sounded plausible enough to get me off, like the time I convinced the highway patrol that the reason I was speeding was because my old car needed to build momentum to make it up the steep grade we were approaching.

The moment I thought "Grand Cayman," however, the entire width of my shoulders was torn into by talons. I was transformed into a common field mouse and was being transported to a nest of hungry eagles.

It occurred to me that my scheme wasn't working. It occurred to me maybe that was the point.

The moment I think "maybe that's the point," the talons release me and now I'm the bird. The wind lifts my wings and then drops me a foot above the river, where I glide in the moonlight.

When the sun comes up, I'm back on my perch, waiting for the voice.

# Journeyman

on the moon the sky is black
I got here on my own

and the days are so much hotter
in the canyons and open spaces
quiet open spaces
like the ache of a bloodless dream

strange I don't recall the names of friends
I am certain there were names
strange I can still wander the woods
though not in current time or place

there is an ancient vine
that has grown since artist times
which I watch for your forever
when it spiraled by I understood
that there always is tomorrow

and the nights are so much brighter
in the canyons and open spaces
quiet open spaces
like the ache of a bloodless dream

on the moon the sky is black
I got here on my own

## Inheritance

I drift in the mountains near the ocean
always at the edge of exhaustion.

Forever slow in the fog of 500 years
I leave parts of me to rest
in redwood grooves
on oak leaves
on granite boulders
in streambeds long gone dry

sad beyond self-will
tranquil beyond pride
forever glimpsing sea and sky
in the light between the trees

# Because

because space is vast
and time infinite
to have spent an hour
in a room with you
in humane discomfort
just the two of us
was a better miracle
than the entropy
and solitude
that awaited us

✝

# Ascension

On that late, late night
when you lie awake
and all that was distortion
suddenly is clear

Rejoice, jaded groundwarmer
your mortal wound
is all bled out and
the time to join us draws near

# Acknowledgments

Special thanks to my editors, Jen Cairns and Greg Dalgleish, for their expert guidance in the evolution and completion of this book.

## About the Author

Douglas Richardson was born on February 20, 1967, in Duluth, Minnesota, and was raised in Camarillo, California. He currently lives in Los Angeles, where he works as a proofreader, editor, novelist, and poet.

## Also by Weak Creature Press:

*Panic Kit* by Laura A. Lionello
*Panic Kit*, Laura A. Lionello's breakout collection of poetry, showcases the author's deft hand and mastery of voice in dealing with universal themes and truths, such as joy, heartache, loss, suffering, and triumph.
**ISBN-10:** 0984242430 (paper)
**ISBN-13:** 978-0-9842424-3-6 (paper)

*Poems for Loners* by Douglas Richardson
In his fourth enigmatic offering, Douglas Richardson employs poems, lyrics, proverbs, letters, and a diary to illuminate the dark lives of loners.
**ISBN-10:** 0984242422 (paper)
**ISBN-13:** 978-0-9842424-2-9 (paper)

*The Corruption of Zachary R.* by Douglas Richardson
Compunction and collusion drive Zachary R. He harbors disillusionment even while performing life's richest rituals: employment, courtship, marriage, and fatherhood. Memories of a neurotic mother and emotionally austere father shade his adult life with ever-darkening tones. Riddled with madness, he reaches out to those who survive him, those whom he loves, those who will seek to do him harm. Their collective path to sanity is neither uncomplicated nor without redemption. Who among them will survive the journey?

**ISBN-10:** 0984242414 (paper)
**ISBN-13:** 978-0-9842424-1-2 (paper)

*Out in the Cold, Cold Day* by Douglas Richardson Poetry chapbook offered exclusively through the publisher. (paper)

All titles offered by Weak Creature Press may be purchased directly from the publisher. Please send an email to **weakcreature@aol.com** for orders or inquiries. Otherwise, you may purchase our titles via online retailers or ask your local bookseller to order them for you.

www.ingramcontent.com/pod-product-compliance
Lightning Source LLC
Chambersburg PA
CBHW061513040426
42450CB00008B/1600